Poems written out of a
longing for peace and
justice —
David Smith-Ferri

WHERE DAYS ARE STONES

Where Days Are Stones

Afghanistan & Gaza Poems
2012-2013

David Smith-Ferri

Foreword by Ann Wright

Haley's
Athol, Massachusetts

Haley's
488 South Main Street
Athol, MA 01331
haley.antique@verizon.net
800.215.8805

Special thanks to Mary-Ann DeVita Palmieri, copy editor.

International Standard Book Number: 978-0-9897667-6-0
Library of Congress Catalogue Number:

Cover photo credits:
Front, Child with a can. Kabul, Afgahnistan. October 2012
Photo by Johnny Barber, oneBrightpearl Photography

Front, background, West Kabul bazaar. October 2012.
Photo by David Smith-Ferri

Back, top, Children near bombed neighbor's home, Gaza, Palestine. November 2012
Photo by Johnny Barber, oneBrightpearl Photography

Back, center, Afghan man in chair. Kabul. October 2012.
Photo by Johnny Barber, oneBrightpearl Photography

Abdulhai, Samia, Kathy, and Zaharoh in the APV house. October, 2012.
Photo by David Smith-Ferri

The longer we listen to one another—with real attention—the more commonality we will find in all our lives.

—Barbara Deming

For the Afghan Peace Volunteers

Contents

Illustrations

Retired United States Army Colonel Ann Wright with, from left, Mary Dobbing, Shane Claiborne, and John Dear in the Afghan Peace Volunteer home in Kabul. December, 2012
—photo by Abdulhai Satar

Its Own Tragic Story

a foreword by Colonel Ann Wright, United States Army (retired)

As I was a part of the United States military-industrial-diplomatic-war complex for almost forty years, I am an unlikely person to write the foreword for David Smith-Ferri's remarkable book of poems concerning war-torn areas. I was in the United States military for twenty-nine years and the United States diplomatic corps for sixteen years. But, in March 2003, I resigned from the United States diplomatic corps in opposition to the United States war on Iraq. Since then I have traveled extensively as a citizen activist to conflict areas, particularly Afghanistan and Gaza, the places David describes in this book.

The people of Afghanistan have been subjected to violence, wars, greed, and corruption for the past four decades. First it was the Soviet invasion of Afghanistan in 1979, followed ten years later by the mujahedeen who, with support from the United States, pushed out the Soviets and then brutally fought among themselves, terrorizing the people of Afghanistan. In 1996, the Taliban dethroned the warlords and began its repressive regime. Twelve years ago, in October 2001, the United States began its invasion and occupation of Afghanistan killing tens of thousands of Afghans in its war on al Qaeda and the Taliban.

The people of Palestine have also suffered violent foreign intervention and occupation. In Gaza and the West Bank, the Israeli military routinely detains, imprisons, and kills Palestinians. The twenty-two day Israeli attack on the people of Gaza in 2009 killed 1440, wounded more than 5,000 and left 50,000 homeless. In November 2012, the eight-day Israeli attack on Gaza killed 162. The United States provides three billion dollars in military aid each year to Israel.

In mid-December 2001, I was on a small team of United States diplomats who reopened the United States Embassy in Kabul. The Embassy had been closed for more than a decade due to instability caused by fighting among warlords and the Taliban. I returned to Afghanistan three times since I resigned as a United States diplomat. The last two times I returned were in December 2011 and December 2012. Like David, I visited the Afghan Peace Volunteers, young Afghans who stand for peace in their country.

Having spent substantial time in both Afghanistan and Gaza, I am deeply moved by David's description through poetry of aspects of the daily life of ordinary citizens in both countries, people who desperately try to survive even as mammoth United States and Israeli military forces hammer them. His poems powerfully capture feelings and emotions of a story that could take thousands of words to flesh out. In a page of poetry, David leaves one with a gut-wrenching view of lives ruled by guns and violence in two war-torn areas of our world.

David writes about direct experiences with people in Gaza and Afghanistan, often creating poems in the voice of Palestinian and Afghan people. He includes their own words and draws us in to a very personal encounter. He also takes the experiences of Kathy Kelly, another great storyteller, who has spent much time in Afghanistan, and expresses them in poetry. Kathy journeys with a group of young Afghans and their mentor, Hakim, as they break down ethnic barriers to live together in Kabul: they decide to live nonviolently in community. Here we have rich and unique insights into Afghan society.

Through poetry, David spells out nightmares and trauma experienced by boys whose parents have been killed in war on Afghanistan. They strive to throw off the past and look to a future they dream will be filled with peace.

Several of David's poems give a glimpse into the lives of women in Afghanistan who desperately try to keep their children alive under the harshest of conditions, where "robbers in the night" come to take children away, robbers that are malnutrition, lack of education, and violence. The women find hope in a sewing project that pays them to make life-saving blankets for those in refugee camps who would die from cold without warm Afghan comforters or duvets. But as critical as life-saving duvets are, the opportunity for the women to meet with other women outside of the house and be paid for their work is equally important to them as they dream of a life without the crushing weight of war and poverty.

In "The Higher You Go," women have to keep moving higher and higher on craggy mountains surrounding Kabul. The higher the small shack home on the mountain, the cheaper its cost. As water and electricity slowly find their way up the mountain, women who have little means are forced higher and higher until they and their children live extraordinarily difficult lives of poverty, disease, and hopelessness. Literally they disappear from society.

In Gaza, lives end and time stands still as missiles hit homes, gardens, agricultural fields, and cars. David captures the horrific moment with "In Gaza, Time Stopped" during the Israeli attack on Gaza unfolding in November 2012.

Every death in conflict has its own tragic story. The poem "More Than a Story" describes the November 2012 Israeli attack on Gaza and the deaths of four women and four children, eight members of the al-Dalu family, during one Israeli air strike that made a crater twenty feet deep. The blast blew apart a three-story building and severely injured many families in the neighborhood. Their lives and hopes were "more than a story." They were the hopes and dreams of any family in Gaza living under daily attacks.

David's poems capture the sense of helplessness of people in the middle of war. Nevertheless shining through David's writing are courage and resilience exhibited by war-ravaged people who hope and believe that wars can end and they can, finally, live in peace.

Ann Wright is a retired United States Army Colonel and former United States diplomat who resigned in 2003 in opposition to the Iraq war. She has traveled to Afghanistan, Gaza, Pakistan, and Yemen to write about the disastrous effects of United States war policies.

AFGHANISTAN

Afghan Peace Volunteers protesting the killing of two Afghan children by a NATO helicopter gunship

—photo by Dr. Wee Teck Young

An International Collaboration: Great Courage and Belief

a comment by David Smith-Ferri

In the fall of 2010 after communicating with American peace activists by Skype and email, the Afghan Peace Volunteers welcomed three members of Voices for Creative Nonviolence to Bamiyan, their home province high in the mountains of north central Afghanistan. A year later in a step that had to take great courage and belief in themselves, the Afghan Peace Volunteers moved to Kabul and rented a house for multi-ethnic Afghan youth to experiment living together. In all likelihood theirs is the first intentional community in Afghanistan seeking ethnic diversity and a commitment to nonviolence in a land where ethnic differences have often led to violence.

Once in Kabul, the peace volunteers began to meet with their neighbors and to assess the needs of their new community. And they began to welcome internationals as guests and friends. When we visited them in October of 2012, their home had become an informal and active community center. Among other things, it offered daily English classes for street youth and other neighborhood children; after-school tutoring in English, math, and Dari, one of Afghanistan's native languages; a women's sewing cooperative whose first project was to organize the production of Afghan duvets (warm comforters) to be distributed to refugee families in advance of winter; a small business incubator; monthly Skype calls with people all over the world; and seminars on current global issues.

People from the neighborhood and from other parts of Kabul dropped by at all times to visit, sharing their perspectives and needs.

Today, the numbers of this group have grown. Having weathered growing pains and crises of self-doubt, the group is maturing in its vision and identity. It has also become more diverse with Hazara, Pashto, and Tajik youth living and working together in a nearly unprecedented way. Equally remarkable, young women participate in many of its activities, and planning for a community of women committed to nonviolence has begun. Their home is a dynamic place where they organize nonviolent actions and where people share a common loathing of war and occupation and a dream of healing and peace. In the poems that follow, I attempt to provide a window on some of these people and their work and on a unique collaboration between the people of Afghanistan and international peace activists during a time of protracted war and occupation fostered and carried out in Afghanistan by the governments of the international activists' home countries.

Women's sewing cooperative distributes duvets they made
—photo by Dr. Wee Teck Young

Beyond Expectations

for Hakim

Beyond all our expectations
and out of all proportion to their circumstances,
a young Hazara man
and a young Pashtun woman
write love letters.
They cannot voice their longing in person,
so they use the Internet.
Each week,
hoping,
they put their words in a bottle
and toss it on global waters.
Currents carry it.

"We moved to Kabul," thirteen-year-old Samia writes,
"because of fighting in Laghman, my home province.
I don't like Kabul because rich people look down on us.
When we first arrived in Kabul,
I used to sweep the streets and alleys
and get twenty Afghanis—thirty-eight cents—for every five houses
along a street.
I don't want to do that again because I want to be a teacher someday.
I was eight years old,
and I would sometimes think,
'Why can't I do what other girls do?'
I thought if I could study like other children,
I would become something someday.
I know everyone has enough problems and can't do much for others.
But I think girls in Afghanistan should study hard
and then help others by teaching them."

Seventeen-year-old Abdulhai echoes and amplifies.
"Every morning in our neighborhood

a hundred men gather on a bridge
looking for work for the day.
When I spoke to them,
their voices were like the voices of people seeking shelter in their
own homes.
They have children at home,
but still they have to stand there for three days
waiting to get one day's work.
This math makes me ill."

Samia writes,
"My mother's main worry is whether we will be safe
and have enough food.
When we don't have enough food,
we know that we'll just have to eat less
and make do.
Sometimes all we have is tea and bread.
If others don't have enough?
We ought to help them if we can."

In Dari, a local language,
the word for bread is naan.
"But naan," Abdulhai says,
"is not our only basic need.
Love is also a basic need.
People need to know that there are others
who care about their survival."

At dawn,
we see the bottles bobbing and tilting
in the wide river of our day,
moving slowly downstream,
sunlight glinting off them.
When we wade into the stream
they bump against our legs and hips.
Some of their words wash onto shore.

Yes, this is courting.
Yes, this is two teenagers asking for love.
But against all expectations,
the letters are written to us.

After-School Class

Every day the children come
in threes and fours
holding hands,
linked like drops of water moving downhill
and pooling in the makeshift classroom
on the ground floor of this house
in western Kabul.
The children of war,
some of them defying gravity
flow up the stairs
to pulse and pool around Abdulhai,
pulling at him,
trying to carry him off.
They climb Boqir like a tree
and nest in his arms, on his shoulders,
sample the fruit of his smiles, his laughter.
They sprout like flowers at Hakim's feet,
gather themselves into bouquets for Firhas and Faiz.

Every day they come like late-afternoon rain
to this desert,
and we drink—
like rainfall in the dark when there is no other sound,
and we listen—
like oxygen-rich air to this mountain city,
and we fill our burning lungs—
like a sea breeze across this land-locked country,
and suddenly we stand on shore
looking out over great distances of salt water.
We see a far-flung horizon
and take its measure.

Deep Listening

All day and into night
the stories come,
rolling into the Afghan Peace Volunteer house in western Kabul,
carrying with them a stench of war,
of gunpowder and burnt flesh,
sounds of boots kicking in doors,
buzz of drones overhead,
dull thud of rifle butts breaking bone and teeth,
children screaming.
One after another,
a long line of stories,
a convoy climbing out of the past
along narrow dirt tracks,
over landmines
and past improvised explosive devices,
rumbling, stumbling,
choking on their own dust and exhaust
but making it.
Malnourished, anemic women with headaches, backaches, dizzy spells,
young men searching the wreckage of the present for a future,
mothers forced to pull their children from school
and put them to work selling candy on the street,
girls pressured to marry against their will,
orphans, street children, drug addicts.
Hakim receives them,
welcoming them,
offering a new perspective,
pointing a way.
He listens
as though theirs were the only stories,
as though each were the first visitor in a year,
an old friend,
a cousin not seen since childhood.

Be patient toward all that is unsolved in your heart and try to love the questions themselves . . . Do not now seek the answers, which cannot be given you because you would not be able to live them.

—Ranier Marie Rilke

Answers

Rilke,
sick in body and heart,
left Paris for the wide expanses of Worpswede,
asking it to heal him.
Absorbing its stillness,
he advised us to abandon our search for answers.
But your grief, Hakim, has led you from the mountains to the city
where you have distilled your life
into a series of questions
that are their own answers.

In a country
shot and stabbed daily,
why more bullets and blades,
why not listen?

In a place where children freeze in winter,
where hunger is the not-so-well-kept secret
of nearly everyone we meet,
where malnutrition is a thief free from pursuit,
why not warmth,
why not food?

Working alongside you
and embodying the questions,
we live the answers, too,
now.

Unspoken Words

We meet with Ziabuddin on the ground floor
in a concrete, windowless room
but with a doorway opening onto a yard
and bright October sunshine resting on its elbows
watching us.
Blind, inarticulate walls listen
as Ziabuddin, leaving most of the story unspoken,
tells us he is from a large Pashtun family
that has trouble feeding itself.
He is twenty
and thinking of leaving for Iran
because he cannot find work in Afghanistan.
Dust stirs and settles like thought,
like the unspoken words
that attend every conversation here in Kabul.

Greeting each other in a customary fashion
with kisses,
other young men join us
and link their stories
one with another.
We stand in a circle.

If I tell you we have come to Kabul
to stand and listen,
will you think,
"All that way
to do something so small,
so ineffectual?"
But all week
these few words
have been waiting for us,
following us like shadows,
rumors, intimations,
the voices of Afghanistan's numberless young,

its countless youth,
half the so-called future of Afghanistan
without a future.
Hakim asks,
"What would you think of forming
a bicycle repair shop
here in the neighborhood,
a cooperative that you would own
and run together?"
The walls lose interest.
The world loses interest.
"Do any of you have experience repairing bicycles
or machines?"
None of them does,
but one young man has a cousin
with a bike repair shop in another neighborhood.
Maybe he'll take some apprentices
and mentor the group.
Hakim tells him, "Contact your cousin.
Meanwhile, we'll keep thinking
about what this might involve
and plan to meet again soon."
The young men attend
not only to his words
but also to Hakim's body,
especially his face and eyes,
probing them,
reading the many words they speak
without speaking.

I have spread my dreams under your feet. Tread softly, because you tread on my dreams.

—William Butler Yeats

Dreaming of Duvets

Haroon has recurring dreams.
Haroon, whose father was killed when he was a boy
and who remembers hunger
preying on him
through every year of his childhood,
gnawing at him,
hunger like a living creature
trapped inside him
and trying to eat its way out
during long winter months
when the store of potatoes ran out.

At night
lying on a concrete floor,
the sounds of the street climbing in his second-story window,
he dreams that someone drops him
from a great height.
In the dream
he free-falls through air,
crashes to hard ground,
and dies.

During the day,
walking the same concrete floor,
he dreams of relief
from the anger and confusion
that pursue him
and of being a photographer, a traveler,
of being something other,
something other than a seventeen-year-old eighth-grader
in occupied Afghanistan.

Haroon is not the only one in this house with recurring dreams.
Faiz, who lost his parents when he was a boy
and whose brother was shot and killed in front of him,
has nightmares, too.
Each night
as he sleeps against the wall a few feet away,
his moans and cries wake me.
By day, he dreams of being a journalist,
of marrying and raising a family,
of a world without borders and war.

Every morning
when they wake,
Faiz and Haroon and their housemates
roll up their blankets and makeshift pillows
in a large sheet.
They sweep the floor
with short-handled straw brooms
purchased in the bazaar.
Two hours later,
the room trades nightmares for daydreams
as it is converted into a classroom
where up to a dozen Afghan women
from the neighborhood meet
six days a week
to learn to sew.
This is how we change things,
they seem to be saying.
And their very presence together in this room
is a direct challenge
to the culture of servitude
that has held them since they were children—
and to war itself
that has fallen over the entire neighborhood
like a net.

"I always wanted to have a job
and earn an income for my family,"
Faribah says,
"but I have never been allowed outside the house.
Coming to this sewing class is the very first time."
Shararah tells a similar story.
"This is the first time
I have been out of the house to learn something.
I have never been allowed outside before."
Around the room, other women echo her words.

They aren't talking about the Taliban
or foreign fighters
imposing Sharia law
but about a culture of male domination
that imprisons women in their homes,
in abusive relationships,
and sentences them to a life at hard labor.

The sewing group has also become a sanctuary,
a place where dreams can be named,
held in public, and nurtured.
These are mothers who dream of feeding their families,
of getting out forever from under the crushing weight of poverty.
Every day, when the women arrive for class,
this dream enters the room with them.
Its voice rings in their laughter
and speaks in the rapid, metallic sounds
of the sewing machines.
It plays on the floor
while they work and talk.
Long after they leave, it lingers.

In January of 2012,
in squalid refugee camps
on the outskirts of Kabul,

dozens of very young Afghan children
froze to death.
Their deaths were as preventable
as the war their families fled.
Malnutrition, poor housing,
and very cold weather conspired
to rob these families of their children.
The women in the sewing group know these thieves
who at night scratch on the doors and windows
of their homes,
visit them in their sleep,
whisper in their ears.
During the day,
these robbers peer from behind their children's eyes.
The women have decided to sew their personal dreams
together with their community's dreams
by making large, warm comforters,
Afghan duvets,
for families living in Kabul's refugee camps
and for widows and single mothers
living in the hills above the city.

And now that it's been said,
now that it has been decided,
we see what can happen
when people have the means
to do something about a problem
that has plagued them.
It's like cresting a hill
or coming over a pass in the mountains.
As though all the energy spent climbing
had been stored
and now released,
propelling the group forward.
Meetings are arranged,
choices made.
"We want to be involved

in all decisions,
especially who participates.
In Afghanistan
we have all learned to cheat and lie.
This project will fail
if we do not run it
with clear rules, oversight,
accountability."

For warmth,
they will fill the duvets with a double layer of wool.
A fee of one hundred Afghanis—about two dollars—
will be paid directly to the seamstress
for each duvet.

Today's meeting ends.
Slowly, slowly the women leave,
saying long, lingering goodbyes to each other.
Their dreams lay at our feet.
All day, we tread softly.

Granite and Obsidian

When these women speak,
they command our attention.

When Shakira tells a story,
our eyes widen.
"The bombs started to fall
on my neighborhood in Kabul,
and I ran.
I was pregnant.
I had three young children hidden in my skirt."

When Golbahar talks,
we sit up, stop what we are doing.
"Afghanistan is a stone
broken in a hundred pieces.
We do not trust anyone.
This is because of war.
And hunger will make your neighbor
steal from you."

The women tell us,
"Warlords and leaders look for their chances.
They divide people through killing.
Civil war could break out again.
It could happen.
Trying to take more power for themselves,
the leaders could do it again."
And we listen.
We take out our notepads and write.

But when the candidates for president
of the most powerful country in the world
speak,
when the make-up artists and barbers and costumers

have finished with them
and they emerge pressed and polished
from the green room, backstage,
to debate,
who listens?
When they stand on their soapbox
and tell us,
"We must overcome our dependence on foreign oil,"
who believes them?
When they talk about "democracy"
and "freedom,"
who can resist laughing?
When they promise the US
will beat the world into prosperity,
when they fail to address climate change,
war in Afghanistan,
poverty in the US,
who is surprised?
When they begin to blur around the edges,
to break up, to pixilate,
to meld with the background,
who feels a loss?
And after they speak, what remains?
When we look down,
our hands are empty.
When we look for their words,
we find they are a fine dust
the wind carries away and scatters.

But these illiterate women astonish us.
Facing us,
they crystallize.
"The assistance that foreign governments bring
goes into the hands of a few very corrupt people

who build homes in Dubai," they tell us.
"None of that help gets to ordinary people.
If you are willing to help,
please come,
hear our stories,
bring the help directly
and don't trust it to the leaders
who are thieves and murderers."

Their words cut and bite us.
"There hasn't been one hour
when I haven't had to worry about finding enough food
for my children
and clothing for them to wear.
Have you ever lived through war?
It is like having to live without oxygen.
We hold our breath all the time.
Every one of us is psychologically harmed.
Tell your government to leave us alone.
We just want work and a semblance of peace
so we can go about our lives and live normally."

Their words are granite and obsidian,
lapis lazuli and feldspar.
We carry them in the palms of our hands.
We finger them.
We feel their sharp edges.
We remember who we are.

Look

for the women in the sewing cooperative

These are not the women
you think they are,
cowering,
voiceless,
rags stuffed in their mouths
by Afghan culture,
feet cut off
by the men in their lives,
their spirit buried alive.

Look at Golbahar,
big-boned, broad-shouldered,
looking you in the eye.

Listen to Faribah:
"We are human beings
with feelings just like you,
and we all want to be free,
to have dignity.
But every family has ten to twelve mouths to feed,
and there are no jobs.
War has caused this disaster.
If it is a matter of our minerals,
tell the US to shift all American citizens to Afghanistan.
We will be happy to change places with you.
Just leave us alone."

Listen to the laughter.

Despite having teeth knocked out
by their husbands
and being locked in their homes,
despite clouds swelling with mortars

and explosions raining on Kabul,
despite dry breasts and vacant larders,
see how they have protected and cared for their children,
how they've cradled families,
shouldered neighborhoods.

Take them away
and everything would fail
and Kabul crash.
Starving, the men who run the city
would eat each other
and die.

All Day

after meeting with the women's sewing cooperative

On shop roofs in the bazaar,
with darkness gathering,
kites descend into the hands of boys
who study the sky
and wish only that they could suspend the sun
just above the horizon.
Across the street from the Afghan Peace Volunteer House,
grated-carrot vendors sprinkle their orange mounds
one last time with water
and cover them with burlap.
Once again, as though it is a welcome visitor,
night throws its long arms around Kabul.

All day, after meeting with you,
after the stories of war and hunger and longing,
after tears, anger, laughter,
it is as though we have been waiting for your return,
expecting to meet you
as we turn from the hallway
into a room
or as we walk down the stairs
into the yard and along the street.
And now
in the quiet moments before sleep,
you come back to us.
Your eyes flash.
Your fierce words explode.

We cannot tell if a star has been born in front of us,
changing the comfortable sky forever
and portending a new order
or if lightning has struck, igniting a forest,

and every word is a torch,
the day itself a kind of night
no sun can quench.

The Higher You Go

after a report by Martha Hennessey and Kathy Kelly

In the oxygen-deprived hills above Kabul,
all the paths are one-way.
The higher you go,
the cheaper the rent.
At their highest reaches,
one-room shanties cling to steep slopes
like old, worn patches on torn clothing.
Snow and wind enter at will.
Whole families,
almost always led by single women,
huddle and hide.
The world has no use for them.
When running water reaches homes
for the first time,
rents are raised
and families have to move up.
Not some fabled economic ladder
but the hillside,
people disappearing
literally
into thin air.

Question

Outside Kabul,
bony, malnourished hills
wake each morning
to the same bitter burden of hunger and heavy toil
playing out on their surface.
A breathtaking view of the city below
adds no sweetness.

While the indifferent world spins through space
and its somnolent nations nurse their dreams
of riches and power,
Kabuli widows and children climb,
summer and winter,
the steep, narrow, stony streets
and crumbling stairways
cut into the scarred hills,
carrying heavy containers of water
on their heads or shoulders
from the bottom of the hill
to their homes.

On a frigid January morning,
led by two young Afghan Peace Volunteers,
Zainab and Umalbanin,
or Banin for short,
we climb the same primitive paths.
Coated in ice, the road resists us.
And even without a heavy load of water buckets,
we gasp and pant
as thin air tries to turn us back.
Hearts hammering,
chests heaving,
we pause
and try to breathe.
But Khoreb,

Banin's aunt,
is standing above
waving to us from her home.
Huffing, we climb the final section of stones
and step, relieved, inside.
At Khoreb's invitation,
her neighbors,
who are all single mothers,
join us.

And once again we listen
while mothers talk about their children.
Once again we hear them say that education,
the "only hope,"
is beyond their means.
"Education is our biggest problem," Fatima says.
"I want all my children to go to school,
but I can afford to send only one.
The others need to work."
Once again we ask the wind and sky
and four directions
how nations can pour their resources into weaponry
and the waging of war.

Resistance

after a report by Martha Hennessy and Kathy Kelly

War is a barbed-wire fence between neighbors,
a hardening of old resentments
and seeding of new ones,
a wall with eyes.

War is a hood, a hole,
a shrinking of horizons,
a dark cloud over your mind
and no silver lining.

War is a weight on your chest,
a pair of hands around your throat,
smoke in your lungs,
thin air.

War is a vortex,
quicksand,
an undertow
sucking you into
itself.

We come to Kabul
and then leave the city
to find resistance.
We climb the hills outside town
to find air we can breathe,
to find someone who has cut holes in barbed wire
and torn down walls.

We stand among forgotten people
to find someone weighty enough to withstand the wind,
to resist the undertow.

We have come to a one-room home
with thin walls and a leaky roof
to find someone who,
when her neighbors fell into a hole,
stood at the lip and called out,
then reached her hand down,
who,
when her neighbor's home was ruined by a storm,
took the family of eight into her own home.
We've come here
to find Khoreb.

The Hard Nut

after a report by Martha Hennessy and Kathy Kelly

Throughout our visit,
Khoreb and her school-age children
shell almonds.
They are so practiced,
so expert at setting the nut,
lifting the rock,
snapping the wrist,
striking the shell at just the right spot
with just the right force
that after a while we hardly notice.
They might as well be knitting
or eating a piece of bread.

Bread is the point.
This is how they feed themselves:
by selling almonds in the market
to buy bread.
And the shells,
their main source of fuel,
provide a thin coat of protection
against the frozen air.
Khoreb throws a handful into a small, iron heater
where we are gathered.
The shells throw off their small flame
and turn to ash.

We, too, want to get to the kernel.
We recall how the US invasion of Afghanistan
was predicated on rescuing women and children,
especially girls,
from servitude,
from a life of hard labor
without education to unlock the chains.

In over eleven years,
the arguments haven't changed.
We listen as Khoreb tells us
she can't afford school fees for her children.
No, it's more than that.
The family can't survive without the income the children earn.
We want to get to the hard nut of it.
There wouldn't be enough food or clothing.
The family would starve
or freeze.
Their lives would be worth less than the scraps of paper
people in Kabul scavenge for fuel.

The children go on shelling almonds.
They want to get to the kernel,
but they are careful to save the shells.

Abdul Ali

Bamiyan boy, ice shaped you.
High in the mountains,
a glacier heaved itself
and sculpted your angular frame,
carving you from rock
rich in copper and iron.
And every day, sunlight struck fire in your face.

Though you don't yet know it,
a council of mountains stood
nodding their heads in approval when you were born.
Every night, they watched as the iron of your youth solidified,
as your volcanic core hummed and burned
to fire passions and the words and actions they birth.

Ali, we have seen you
like any adolescent,
translucent and amorphous,
on the periphery
of adult conversations and meetings,
waiting for your molten identity to harden.
You know it.

Do you also know
how you grow in stature,
how you crystallize before us
when you speak from your experience
and when you describe the nonviolent "Two Million Friends" cam-
paign
to visiting youth?

Hazara boy from Bamiyan
here in the capital city,
studying late at night,
meeting with internationals,
visiting India,

a river runs in you
rushing down mountainsides
over boulders,
twisting and gurgling,
sliding beneath branches and leaves,
joining other waters and widening,
nurturing trees and birds and berries.
River of words—
river of dreams—
river of actions and associations,
carrying you where ice never traveled
where ice never dreamed,
where ice cannot follow.

All That We've Ever Had

for Abdulhai

Child of windy heights,
of swirling snow
and snow-bit broken rocks,
come down,
come down to Kabul.

We know some of the stories:
how the terrified women
found your infant body
half-frozen
and held you over the flame-licked embers,
their hands beating death back,
their arms holding on to the light
even while night lingered above the Hindu Kush
and cradled your village in darkness.

Three years later
your older brother, Khamad Jan,
nimble as a goat,
carried you on his shoulders
sidestepping rocks,
keeping his balance,
somehow bringing you to safety.
He cupped the small flame of your life
in his hands
even as the Taliban raided your village
bringing a version of darkness
that defied the dawn.

As though remembering the arms that held it,
the hands that shielded it,
that light has grown, Abdulhai.
We've seen you burn,

you a torch in the world's night,
a soul longing for an end to war,
for a way out of a future bound
wrist and ankle
by guns and poverty.
But now, as you have turned inward
following a track you must follow,
winding down into the earth,
into your self,
the dimming of that flame is a palpable loss
to us all.

Your smile, your contagious laughter
have led us.
We've felt your arm around our shoulders,
and long to feel it there again.

But the questions have all changed
and even stories from your childhood
with their dramatic resolutions
provide no answers.

Still,
looking for signs of back doors, side passages,
an escape route you can follow out of the catacombs,
we probe them for clues.

Finding none,
we offer all that we've ever had—
our hands,
our outstretched arms,
our feet standing beside you.

Faiz Ahmad

Snow fell on your childhood.
Day and night,
frozen water descended,
a whiteout
coating roofs,
blotting out roads,
piling up against the outer walls of your home,
covering trees and erasing their colors.
Flake by flake by flake—
who could count them?
They fell at the feet of your parents
and alongside your sleeping brother
and buried them
forever.

Maybe the snow came from trees,
swooping down like an owl,
a white owl with iron claws.
Maybe it came from the mountains,
like an avalanche
or snarling like a pack of wolves
or from the sky,
from blocks of ice
shattered and dropping like daggers into the valley,
into your home.
You couldn't tell.

Later
there was only silence—
silence and emptiness.
You blinked your eyes
in a world without your parents,
without your brother.

And the earth kept spinning.
Even with your parents dead
and your brother killed in front of you,
day followed night,
birds opened their mouths,
stars danced across the sky,
and you heard no music, no song.

But to someone from whom so much was taken,
so much afterward must have been given.

How else explain today,
fourteen years later,
your voice singing
when you enter the house,
your body dancing with Issa
in the kitchen?

How else explain
your voice in public
denouncing revenge,
your body on the line
in Jalalabad, Parwan, Kapisa
promoting a youth peace movement?

How else,
unless others lent you
their voices,
their bodies?

Small Things

October 29, 2012 as Hurricane Sandy approaches

In every major media outlet,
storm centers appear,
storm experts issue advisories,
and late in the afternoon, our eyes
imprinted with the swirling, counter-clockwise colors
of hurricane monitor maps,
ache from the glare of television screens.
Soon we know the wind speed at ground level
in cities we've never been to:
Hartford, Providence, Portland.
And in New Jersey,
where the storm's center threatens landfall,
people head east to the ocean
to watch the waves
leap to shore
like long jumpers.

But you've been imprinted by too many storms, Ghulamai,
to watch and whistle at their approach,
the current storm taking your father away to Iran
to look for work
and taking you out of school.
The wounds are too fresh.

We sometimes wonder
what could have survived.
And when we search the Afghan Peace Volunteers house for your
words,
we find they have dissolved
and left only your exemplary, quiet presence
bowing in prayer,
sweeping hallways and stairwells,
cooking meals,
scrubbing pots.

We sometimes wonder
how anything can survive
nearly four decades of war.
Here in Kabul, small things astonish us:
a kite pulling at its string,
a fruit tree near a house
and birdsong high in its branches,
your smile greeting us
every morning.

We Know

Ghulamai tells a story

We all know
the metal gate
that separates our yard from the street
is a thin skin.
At any time
violence could extend its claws
and draw blood.

This morning,
I loaded a rusty wheelbarrow with bulging trash bags
and leaning into it
rolled it across the yard,
through the gate,
and onto a pocked, unpaved street,
heading for the neighborhood dumpster.
The sun shone on another dusty day in Kabul.
Nothing could have been more ordinary
or more forgettable
until four young Pashto boys on bicycles approached.
"Can we go through your garbage here,"
they asked me,
"before you dump it?"
Bent to their work, they pulled out scraps of stale flatbread
and crumpled pieces of paper for fuel.
One of them pointed to a nearby residence
where a member of Parliament lives.
"Look at how the people in that castle live," he said,
"and how we live."
The boys finished their sorting
and thanked me.
As they walked away,
I saw that a thin metal gate stands between us,
and they are already bleeding.

Bulwark

Early each morning
before school
before breakfast
before the sun's feathered fingers
stroke the face of the mountains outside Kabul,
Ali, Ghulamai, Faiz, and I gather to stretch and exercise
on the rough, thin, red carpet
covering the concrete second floor hallway.

We groan and gasp.
Sets of pushups, planks, leg lifts, sit-ups,
a series of deep-knee bends that Faiz always leads.
Everyone laughs as jumping jacks devolve
into a mad and chaotic dance.
Joking, "I think there are two baby boys in there now,"
Faiz shows off his belly fat.
The rest of us, thin as boards, applaud.
Feinting, ducking, jabbing,
Ali flexes his muscles, balls his fists in front of him,
and pretends to box with me.
Ghulamai strains.
Our enthusiasm far exceeding our accomplishments,
we slap and cheer each other.

It isn't the exercise that matters.
We play at building muscle,

but it's no game this morning ritual
rehearsal
practice, practice—
this building friendship
as a bulwark
against war.

Even the Oceans

Ali,
it may appear that we do not need you,
that we are a circle
complete without you,
or like others,
that we only want something from you—
pictures, stories, quotes for our newsletter.

No. If we are not sisters and brothers,
if we are not points in the same line
reaching for the same goal,
particles of the same beam of light
traveling without end,
letters in the same word,
words in the same message,
we are lost.
We need you
as we need each other.
You are one of us,
and despite the distance,
when we think of ourselves,
when we gather here in the US,
it is as though you are here, too.
Knowing this,
even mountains
even continents
even oceans cannot separate us.

Even time bends.
When you appeared
alone, empty-handed,
outside the airport in Kabul to meet me,
no one else could see
you carried the past with you.

With the strength of your smile,
with the long reach of your eyes,
you pulled it into the present,
and the intervening two years were as hours or days.

Ali,
I learned last night
that you had decided
after a flare-up
to leave the group,
and already the distance between us has increased.
The mountains straighten their backs,
the oceans gather themselves to leap,
and my hand,
which only days ago held yours,
mourns the loss of your fingers.

Pole Vault

the Afghan Peace Volunteers speak

The world has contracted.
In Bamiyan and Dai Kundi,
in Maidan Wardak and Mazar,
we measured ourselves
against mountains and wind.
We could walk forever
without coming up against a fence.

Now
in Kabul,
it is dangerous to leave the city.
The war closes in on us,
blocks our way
like a wall.

Every day now
in class
at the Afghan Peace Volunteers house,
we measure ourselves
against English.
And in a house where Pashtuns
and Tajiks and Hazaras
bump up against each other,
we measure ourselves against our dreams.
We will use them as a vault.

No Trace

Mohammad speaks

I'll tell you what it's like where I come from.
If the mountains fell on us,
if two of them chose to squeeze and grind us
like kernels of wheat between stones,
they would laugh while crushing us into flour.
This is what it is like in my district
in Dai Kundi province.
The days are stones,
grinding us.

Dai Kundi is not so far from Kabul,
but if you live there,
it is as though the central government doesn't exist.
Strongmen rule.
Guns rule.
There are three competing militias.
Only last night,
a strongman kidnapped a person from enemy territory
and imprisoned him in his home.
No one can do anything about this.

And the United States?
The internationals?
Do they know we are hungry
and our children malnourished?
Do they know we have no electricity?
Do they know the nearest clinic is eight hours away?
Do they know last month my cousin died in childbirth?
They don't even know we exist.

We are chaff carried away by the wind.
We make no sound in the world.
We leave no trace.

Not in This World

youth in Dai Kundi speak

We could never have expected this.
Not in this world
or any other grown so small.
Bombs, we expected.
Bullets, yes,
and broken promises.
The threat of violence—
a mountain hemming us in,
shrinking our world.
And the word "No"
graffitied on its flanks.
The word "No" repeated endlessly,
echoing in every corner of our valley,
soaking into us,
becoming a part of our identity.
The word "No" a band restricting our hearts.

We expected the roads to grow eyes and hands
and carry guns,
and we weren't surprised
when the head of our youth group
canceled your visit
because traveling between Bamiyan and Dai Kundi
had become too dangerous,
even for pilgrims.

But when your gifts arrived—
leather cellphone pouches
cut and sown by your own hands

and with the Dari symbol for "peace"
stitched into them,
one for each of us—
our hearts swelled,
and we saw a way
through the mountains,
open and free.

Global Days of Listening

for Doug

Afghan youth speak

This is what we know.
Before memory,
weathered faces loomed above us,
women rose at night to keep us in this world,
rough hands held us against cold and wind.
The world was sun-washed and vulnerable.
We did not choose this place.
It chose us.

This is what we remember.
The voices of our parents
coming to us from their childhoods,
and our grandparents speaking
and their grandparents, too,
and older voices we could not identify
from a time when they were young parents
trying to protect their children
from war and hunger.
Their voices traveling all that way,
coming to us like starlight,
carrying pictures, messages, stories
from other times.
Every day they spoke to us.
We heard them echoing in canyons
off red limestone walls,
issuing from newly plowed soil,
falling with apples from trees,
moving like a wind through pomegranate orchards,
like the breathing of the earth itself at night,
condemning war
and weapons
and foreign interference in our country

and the people who profit from it.
And our heads ached with the weight of their words.
And their words became ours.
And we could not silence the voices in our heads,
our own voices,
screaming or pleading,
locked in our heads,
clawing at our skulls,
desperate for a way out.

We did not choose these memories.
They chose us.

And in our own childhood,
the rumble of drones
and the high-overhead roar
of modern fighter planes reverberate
alongside the crash of mortars from previous wars.
The crack of suicide bombers
and rocket-propelled grenades
collide with the explosions of landmines,
laid before we were born.

All of it trapped for years
behind the high stone walls of our minds
until Doug and Mark,
with fingers and hands
and a tool called Skype,
tunneled in.
Every month now,
our words
like bees from an underground nest,
stream out into the world
to probe and question it.
Every day they return with gifts.

Sitting with Raz Mohammad - I

Every chance he has,
Raz sits with me.
He speaks in symbols.
"I do not consider myself first and foremost as Pashtun
but as Afghan,
and everyone else is my brother.
I see it this way:
one arm is Pashtun,
the other is Tajik.
One leg is Hazara,
the other is Uzbek.
And when one part is injured,
the whole body suffers.
My father tells me
that when he was young,
we had no problems
among ethnic groups.
The problem came with foreign intervention."

Sitting with Raz Mohammad - II

To convey his urgency,
Raz uses his body
as much as his voice.
We sit on the floor
cross-legged,
facing each other.
He leans in
until we are only inches apart.
He pleads with his eyes.
He wraps his hands and arms
around his words
and offers them, gifts, to me.
He nods questioning at the end of sentences,
his eyes widening,
his face smiling,
asking my understanding, agreement.
He wants someone to listen.
He wants someone to understand.
He wants someone to see that
"the US project
of targeting Pashtuns
over the last eleven years
has been a problem."

Sitting with Raz Mohammad - III

"In the cities,
it may feel good
to have a large US military presence,
but people in the provinces,
people in the villages
do not feel good.
In the provinces,
people cannot live their dream.
What is their dream?
Their dream is a country at peace
where they can sit down with their families,
safe in their homes,
drink tea,
and enjoy their children
and grandchildren.
But they are caught between the US
and anti-government forces.
From bases in the cities,
the US carries out missions in the provinces.
Both sides demand loyalty,
and the people are caught in the middle.
Whichever way they turn,
they are attacked from behind."

No Formula

Raz Mohammad's sister speaks

Even though it was a stranger
who had never been here before,
the bomb that killed my son's father
had a map of our land in its mind
and a formula for finding it
among all the properties
in this remote and mountainous place.
It didn't know
the number of stones in the low wall
that runs along the border
with our neighbor's land
or the markings on the hands
that built it,
but it knew the wall at first sight.
And though it hadn't been raised nearby
and had never walked the dusty roads
in our village
with the sun like a weight on its shoulder
and sweat running down its neck,
still, it had a formula for finding
the path that leads to our door.

And when the bomb had destroyed our home
and killed my husband,
the US military
had a formula
for calculating his worth
and compensating us.
Less, I am told,
than the cost of a necklace
or a swimming pool
in America.
Less, it goes without saying,

than the cost of the bomb
or the pilotless plane
that dropped it.

Our son was a baby
when the missile struck our home.
Now he is growing up without a father.
There is no formula for this.

Our son was a baby
when the missile killed his father.
Later, when he was older,
later when he asked,
"What happened to my father?"
we did not know what to say.
There is no formula for this.

Graduation Speech

**on the eve of graduating from a two-year engineering college
Mohammad Jan and Raz Mohammad speak**

"We know the numbers,"
Mohammad Jan says.
"160,000 Afghan students will apply
for 40,000 places in higher education.
But unless you slip behind the numbers,
you won't see
what we see."

"The entrance exams," Raz adds,
"are meaningless.
You cannot get a seat in a four-year school
unless you have money
or a Member of Parliament sponsors you.
And it is the same with work.
You have to buy a job.
The more you pay,
the better the job."

"Our parents' generation has failed us,"
Mohammad Jan states.
"We are not blind,
but we can't see the next step.
We have legs,
but we can't go forward."

"I'll tell you what we do see," Raz says.
"Other countries advancing
while ours stands still.
Youth in other countries opening doors,
testing themselves,

building something,
part of the life of their nation,
while here we cannot reach the knob,
we cannot even approach the doorway.
Our arms hang at our sides,
our hands are empty.
We hate it."

"Afghan youth,"
Mohammad Jan tells me,
"are saying:
'We've gone to school for fourteen years
and there's no job for us.'
So they go home
and join the Taliban.
The US has been here for eleven years
trying to defeat the insurgency,
trying to erase their numbers.
But when we look at our country,
the insurgency is all we can see."

What We Know

Raz Mohammad describes an Afghan Peace Volunteer protest

Bad news travels quickly
even in Afghanistan
along perilous, broken roads,
even over mountains
in winter.
When we washed out into the street,
to join our friends in protest—
a small wave of young Afghans
leading two cows
and holding our handmade signs—
people in Kabul already knew
about the two young boys in Uruzgan.
They already knew that six-year old Toor Jan
and seven-year old Odood
were breadwinners for their fatherless family,
and that their widowed mother counted on them
to gather fuel and tend livestock,
to help make yogurt and cheese
and sell it in the market.
They already knew that a NATO helicopter gunship
had killed the boys while they were collecting firewood.

They knew something else, too.
They knew the weaponry of war
had outgrown its makers long ago,
that somehow the helicopter,
not the pilot,
was giving orders.

When we stood together—
Hazara, Pashtun, Tajik,
young men and young women,
girls and boys—
we knew something, too.
We knew ourselves.
Against doubt, our signs declared it.
We are those two children.
We believe it.
And we know that war asks us to forget.

An explosion heard across Kabul on Tuesday morning appeared aimed at killing a prominent ethnic Hazara politician as he was traveling in his armored convoy. The politician survived, but at least three civilians were killed...and thirty were injured.

—New York Times, June 18, 2013

The Bomb

An unnatural thing.
Designed without eyes or ears
or legs,
buried on the side of a road,
a thing without heart or lungs,
a thing without appetite.
A thing with a small mind
but with a hundred hands,
every one of them holding a knife.

Today

Unlike a thunderclap
announced by dark clouds and lightning,
or a tornado
preceded by a drop in air pressure
and a sickening green cast to a troubled sky,
the bomb exploded without warning.

The poker-faced day
like any other
had sat across the table from us,
its cards close to its chest,
daring us to make a play.

It was a high-stakes game we didn't choose.
And we had almost forgotten we were in it
when the day laid down its hand.

We didn't intend to go to the bomb site. But as we had already planned a day to clean the neighborhood streets, it became quite natural to clean around that area and along the street. We recognize the pain caused by the bombing, both the loss of lives and injuries, and also the damage to the environment. We ask for healing. We want the place to be healed. We also want to make a statement: whatever it is the powers that be want for Afghans, we want something different. We don't agree with their violent methods.

—Afghan Peace Volunteers, June 21, 2013

Statement

After a roadside bomb exploded
shattering every window in our home
and shaking the foundations of this neighborhood,
our wild hearts kicked and reared
and pulled at their tethers in terror.
We cut their ropes,
and when they leaped the corral fence,
we followed them to the bomb site
only a few dozen meters away.
With straw brooms,
we swept glass and garbage off the street.
And for a moment,
in silence,
our hearts beating in sync,
we circled the bomb crater
remembering those who were killed or injured
and also in silent protest.

Afterward,
without any need for ropes or tethers,
we led our hearts home.

Ready to Bloom

People ask if it would be better.
Maybe, they say, it would be better
not to think or write about it,
to leave the page blank,
not to write even one word,
to keep every image and thought
locked in its private cell, beneath the soil, dormant.
Better yet,
heave more dirt and rock on top,
pour a concrete cap
and seal it underground
like nuclear waste.

Easier, certainly.
Easier not to picture Logar Province,
its name from the Pashto
meaning Great Mountain.
The Logar River a knife and hand slipping out from under ice
high in the mountain
and cutting a gash in its face,
flashing and slicing through clefts and narrow rock passages
it created.
Then dropping its blade
and carrying silt in muscular arms
until opening out in the flat valley
and unrolling a green tapestry
in an otherwise gray-brown landscape.

Better not to remember the Greco-Buddhist culture
that flourished in Logar two thousand years ago,
the busy monastery, its gilded statues,
the stupas,
the prayers and ceremonies.
Better not to remember the caravans splicing cultures and countries,

carrying spices,
miles of woolen textiles and cotton,
precious metals and gemstones,
the merchants and artists, the scientists,
all the new ideas moving through Logar along the Silk Road.

Better not to remember
weapons and fuel for Mujahideen fighters
following this same route,
during the Soviet occupation
or that Logar was the most heavily bombed province
at that time.
"Everywhere in Logar Province,"
said Swedish journalist Borge Almqvist,
"the most common sights,
except for ruins,
are graves."

And maybe we shouldn't utter a word
today
about the NATO air attack
in Logar's Baraki Barak district.
Bombs falling from forty thousand feet
on Basir Akhunzada's home
where eighteen people were celebrating a wedding.
Better perhaps
not to imagine the songs, music, laughter,
the colorful wedding garments,
the dancing,
their small home dwarfed by a landscape
and by war
but nonetheless bulging with dreams,
with promise,
everyone at the celebration with a hand on the plowshare of time
turning a furrow in the future
and seeding it.

Better not to think of the bomb
uninvited
unwelcome
breaking in
flattening the home,
ending every life in it,
poisoning the future,
and signing its name
for all to read
in its toxic soil.

But the thought has already pushed up through ground
at Raytheon and Lockheed,
at General Dynamics and Boeing,
in their warehouses and offices and factories,
among engineers,
among managers,
among technicians.

In the bomb bay of every F-16 and helicopter gunship,
of every Reaper Drone,
it waits,
the tight-fisted bud of a lethal flower
ready to bloom.

Stepping In

I
Farzana knew there were risks.
Every day was a risk.
For women in Afghanistan,
merely stepping outside—
not to mention acting in the theater—
was a risk.

II
Farhad only wanted to be with Farzana.
She would be how he steered into the future.
She would be how he forgot.
And the years of not knowing,
not seeing a way,
would recede.
In a country where no one could be trusted,
where the possibility of trust
had been taken, tortured, and dumped in the road,
he would start over with her.
Together, they would learn something new.
In the cement and dust of their world,
their trust would be a flower between them.

And in a city without joy,
why not teach her to swim?
Farhad had only wanted to teach Farzana to swim.
So they met at the public lake in Kabul,
and in the oppressive summer heat,
they entered the shallow water.
Someone pointed a finger, a chin in their direction,
someone objected, someone sounded an alarm.
How quick and common alarms are in our city, Farhad thought,
but surely this isn't serious.
We will move away along the shoreline.

Someone pulled out a gun.
Farzana thought of him as a jailer,
one of the people who wanted to imprison her—
in a house, in a marriage she didn't want,
in unending heavy labor,
in servitude to a man.
The solid bed of the lake fell away,
the wind kicked up, the water rose.

It was a stranger who threatened them,
one person waving a gun,
commanding wind and water.
And it was other strangers who stepped in
up to their chins,
people used to treading water but tired of it,
people who knew how bad, in an instant, could become irrevocably
worse,
how blood will mix with water and ruin it.
People who knew what they were doing
when they stood between the young couple
and the man with the gun.

The lake bed solidified
the wind fled,
and Farzana learned to swim.

National Priorities

In the taxi
with Farhad and his mother-in-law
but without a word of Dari,
I am deaf and dumb
but not blind.
Still, I lose track
of the government buildings we pass.
The eighteen-story Ministry of Telecommunications—
the tallest building in the country—
the opulent Presidential Palace,
Ministry of Finance,
Ministry of Foreign Affairs,
the Iranian and French Ministries of Cultural Affairs,
numerous embassies.
Every one impenetrable,
a fortress
with tall, concrete blast walls
topped by pikes and razor wire.
In some cases,
if you can get past the first wall,
another awaits.
Even the dilapidated national zoo is protected
by fences and wire.

In front or alongside us as we drive,
a family on a motorcycle
weaves in and out of traffic.
The man drives,
holding on and steering with both hands,
his legs astride the seat.
Behind him,
his wife maintains her modesty
by riding sidesaddle.
In her arms,
an infant.

Balanced on a pinnacle,
she is moving at thirty-five miles an hour
This is not a circus act.
It is transportation.
They could be headed to a relative's house
or a hospital.
They could have a meeting with President Karzai.
Whatever their destination,
they risk the avalanche of Kabul traffic.
The mother wraps both arms around their infant.
With the five thin fingers of her left hand,
she clasps the cotton fabric of her husband's jacket.
She wants to be blast wall and razor wire
for her newborn child.

Roses

In Afghanistan,
constant reminders of our frailty,
mortality.
We wait for a taxi in Pul-e-Surkh
at the dusty junction of two main roads.
Beneath an overpass,
the Kabul River limps along
weighed by its burden of trash,
failing to cleanse itself of traumatic memories
as I try to forget Shakira's story
about having to walk with her children
past scores of bodies
dumped and piled at this very intersection
during the civil war in the early 1990s.
A sight she will never forget.

From there
the taxi ride across lawless, laneless Kabul
is a little too much like white-water rafting:
bruising and right on the edge of terrifying.
Slamming us against the doors and dashboard,
a power we cannot control
propels us down the road.
Seatbelts remain a thing of the future.
Downtown finally, we stand on the wide sidewalk
outside the Ministry of Foreign Affairs
waiting for Asif's friend to join us,
someone with an in
who can help us acquire the foreign business license
we've been seeking for months.
I do not notice the plants
growing in tightly spaced boxes
lining the curb in front of us
until Farhad asks me its name.

"Roses."
I see only the plant,
its thorny, bony branches,
like fingers
holding pink petals.
I do not see the eight-foot, concrete planter boxes
until Farhad wants me to see them.
"They are here," he says,
"to stop suicide bombers
in trucks."

Into the Future

Farhad and I exchange few words
during the half- hour walk
from the Afghan Ministry of Foreign Affairs
to the Iranian Embassy,
where we pick up his mother-in-law,
to a place beyond that
where we can hail a taxi.
It isn't a lack of friendliness or interest
but the absence of common language.
And I am sure he has no intention of frightening me
as we pass the US Embassy
and he says,
in his laconic way
without introduction or explanation,
"This is the most dangerous street in Kabul."
I am sure he is being hospitable
by informing me,
but we both know there is nothing we can do.
Those few words
and the simple act of walking together
on this street
unite us.
I look at the cars and trucks
and observe their drivers.
I can see nothing beyond this moment.
We continue on foot
into the future.

Against My Will

A knot of young Afghan men
smoke cigarettes,
cluster alongside a lamp post.
Joking and laughing,
they point at me.
They stare.
They leer.
In a foreign country,
on an unfamiliar street,
in bright sunshine,
I am being undressed
in public
against my will.

Ask Anyone

for Natiq Hamidullah

They have taken the torturers.
They have taken the jailers.
They have taken the rapists.

And didn't we want this,
hadn't we longed for it
as we longed for food, for sleep?
Wasn't it air and water,
wasn't it a dream we could not live without?

They have taken the butchers,
the mutilators,
the decapitators.

And aren't we breathing again,
delighting in the free movement of our chests
up and down,
in love with our nostrils, our throats?

They have taken the thieves,
and aren't we out in our yards astonished by the day?
Where had it been all these years?
Aren't the stars that haven't sung in memory singing again?

They have taken the arsonists,
and aren't we grateful?
Aren't we gathering in the streets
to chant our thanks?

Yes, they have taken them.
The Americans came and took them.
They took the strongmen, yes,
and put them in palaces.
They took the warlords
and made them the government.

Market

Before the first rays of sun
have begun to climb down
the snowy mountains
north and east of the city,
the market here in western Kabul
blinks its eyes,
yawns, stretches,
crawls out from under its blankets,
shivers,
and rouses itself
in the half light of a December dawn.
A vendor blows on his hands
before pulling a burlap covering
off a mound of shredded carrots,
itself a sunrise.
Shop owners greet each other
while unlocking the barred gates to their stores.
Soon the first pedestrians come,
walking quickly,
hands in pockets,
shoulders hunched.
They are followed by men on bicycles
or horses,
their faces wrapped in scarves.
And giggling school children
in uniforms.
And huffing donkeys pulling carts
loaded with onions and potatoes,
pomegranates, and greens.
And cars and trucks and SUVs.
All day and into the evening,
it will ring with voices and hoofs,
engines and horns.
Their echoes will whisper
in stairwells and hallways,
in teacups and kitchens,

in drawers and dreams,
a charm against the empty night,
a banked fire against the cold.

Avalanche

an Afghan army commando speaks

I was based in Kandahar.
We carried out raids side by side with American commandos
in the middle of the night
when the enemy was vulnerable.

There were two types of night raids.
One where the mission was to kill everyone
and the other where the goal was to kill
or capture a specific person.

Once we set up an ambush
high in the hills above a road
where it came through a narrow canyon.
Our group split up.
On each side of the road
we had light guns in the middle
flanked by heavy guns.
And snipers outside them
in case anyone tried to escape.
Our mission that day was to destroy everything.
The command to shoot
was followed by a full minute of intense firing.
We poured everything on them.

Convoy

an Afghan army commando speaks

A convoy is a spectacle.
You can't miss it.
Even the dead sit up, take notice.
And moving through rural areas
was like driving through a cemetery.
Death was nearby,
underground
but trying to break through
and take you.

In a convoy,
you try to follow in the exact path
of the truck in front of you.

Unless there is no truck in front.

We were the lead truck
in a convoy in Kandahar province.
Motorcycles were in front
checking for improvised explosive devices—IEDs,
but the truck driver was careless
and didn't wait for clearance.
We crossed a muddy area
and hit an IED.
Death didn't take me that day,
but the driver was killed.

The American trucks were further back.
Afghans always led convoys.

Forgetting Who I Am

Westerners, obviously.
And walking through the commercial district streets
in Kabul,
Kathy and I may have looked more like a married couple
with money to spend
than penny-pinching peaceniks
looking for a travel agent and a way out of Afghanistan
that wouldn't empty our pockets.

Still, stepping as directed through glass doors
into an office building
with large, exterior advertisements of commercial airlines,
we knew who we were.
Even as we were ushered into a small private room
without computers,
given tea,
and asked to wait,
even though there wasn't yet a single sign
that this was a travel agency or an airlines ticket office,
we still believed we were about to meet
an Emirates sales representative
who would untangle the knotted string
of our travel itinerary.
Desperation breeds faith.
And, anyway, in Afghanistan
appearances can fool you.

But when two gentlemen joined us,
laid a locked box on the table between us,
and asked,
"What gems are you interested in?"
our eyes widened,
and our minds galloped.

Even after we had explained and apologized
twice,
even as we were standing up and saying
"Thank you, but ..."
they still wanted to know if we would like to see
the emeralds.

And even after we stepped shaking our heads
into the bright, seen-it-all sunshine
our semi-precious, sapphire eyes refracting the light,
laughter breaking out of our tight lips,
a small piece of me remained behind
in the back room,
sipping tea
and watching the men watching me
as they opened the box of green jewels.

Bear Hug

A young Afghan man
will sometimes greet a friend
with a bear hug,
his hands facing each other and locked together
behind the other's back,
his arms constricting like a python.
It can be both playful and competitive—
impromptu Greco-Roman wrestling
that might not end until one person is lifted off the floor
or has the air squeezed out of him.

Light as a flag,
I was raised off the ground many times,
and I always took it as a gesture of friendship
and affection.

As we were saying our goodbyes
on the day we departed,
Nao Roz, a small man himself,
lifted me off the floor,
and with his customary big smile
and bright, expressive eyes behind thick glasses,
said something in Dari.
Over the previous weeks,
because of the absence of a common language,
we'd spoken little.
And so I was surprised when Faiz translated,
"David is so small around the chest,
like a boy,
but it is what is inside that matters,
and his heart is big."
All the way home,
across mountains and oceans,
during endless lines

and hours in airports,
his words marked me,
wrapping me like a scarf
and adding color
and character
and identity.

Ready to Write

At first, no movement.
Despite daily encounters
with Afghan people
and absorbing their stories,
no poetry.
No words churning in underground chambers
under increasing pressure
and clamoring to be released and heard,
no bright and molten images projected on my consciousness.
No sudden, unexpected visitors,
until, en route home,
somewhere over Czechoslovakia,
somewhere along the volatile strike-slip fault
where mind and heart meet and grind,
the ground shifted.
Wave after wave of sobs,
though not for the Afghan people I'd met.
Head in hands,
I shook with anger,
with a child's anger and self-pity
when faced with hard and daunting work.
A tantrum.
At first, the only word
in my head was No!
Molten refusal.
No, I refuse to do the hard work of writing poetry,
of returning over and over
to the stories Afghan people told us.
I refuse to step into the vault of memory,
with all those tongues,
all those mouths,
all the eyes flashing
or pleading.
I refuse to listen to women

who fled under siege with their children,
whose breasts ran dry,
who chewed nuts and fed the mash to fledgling infants
as a bird would do.
I refuse to stand again and again
in the park with Mohm'a Jan,
to look into his eyes
as he describes the caverns and underground passages Afghan youth
must negotiate,
the many side tunnels that lead down but not out,
and the one clear route to the surface
exiting through a doorway labeled "Afghan police,"
labeled "Afghan National Army,"
labeled "local militia."
I will not sit on the floor for days or weeks with Raz
while he describes the drone attack that killed his brother-in-law,
leaving his sister a widow and his newborn nephew fatherless,
the only response from the US
an offering of money in his place.
I do not want to hold that tension
until the fault slips
and the words flow.

And then the dreams
like aftershocks.
Always the room without walls,
the bright, clinical, artificial light,
the featureless person suspended from somewhere above
and wrapped like a mummy
head to toe in white bandages.
In the foreground,
a pair of arms and shoulders enters the picture,
the back of a head,
a single pair of hands.
One arm reaches behind the person,
one hand finds the center of the back

and pulls,
as in an embrace.
But the other hand,
the other hand holds a weapon
shaped like a pistol,
and at the end of its barrel
a four-inch, red-hot metal plate.
Again and again it is pressed through the bandages
into flesh concealed within.
The person wrapped in bandages writhes.
I have no voice and no body.
I cannot scream.
I cannot even shout my horror.
I cannot stop the torture
until finally, unable to bear it,
I rip myself out of the brightly lit dream
into the dark of wakefulness.
Tongue in mouth,
pen in hand,
and face to face with the blank, black book of consciousness.

If dreams are poetry,
if poems, like dreams, have their own integrity,
their own will,
an internal compass guiding them—
lead on.

Dream

On the day in early winter
when Linda arrived in Kabul
carrying warmth,
and Kathy and Josh left for shipwrecked Gaza,
gale force winds still driving the sea onto that land,
I dreamed of a crossing,
a bridge over a bay
and most of us in a large, heavy vehicle,
strapped in,
protected by thick glass and steel.
But three friends,
two women and a man,
walked in front of us
when without warning
the water leapt,
sweeping the deck of the bridge
and hurling our friends a hundred feet
into the sea.
It was only later,
after the first wave of grief had retreated,
after their bodies,
cold as the water,
had been found
that we realized we could have been with them.

TRANSITION

Afghan Peace Volunteers at their home in Kabul
—photo by Dr. Wee Teck Young

Raz Mohammad in the Afghan Peace
Volunteer home in Kabul
—photo by David Smith-Ferri

Madleen Kulab, the only professional
fisherwoman in Gaza
—photo by Maher Alaa, with thanks to Josh Brollier

Tipping the Scales

September 21, 2012 • Global Days of Listening

Equinox. And the scales are balanced:
day and night nearly even everywhere.
Before it summits Red Mountain east of Ukiah,
slanting sunlight rolls over the rocks
and pours into north-running folds in the hills
turning remnant pockets of mist and fog gold,
and again we hear it,
Anees's voice from Gaza
as we heard it,
warm and intelligent,
in a cold hotel room in Bamiyan
nearly two years ago,
Anees's voice weighing the effects of war.

"I work with kids at the Rachel Corrie Center
because this is the work that I love.
I want children here to be happy.
I don't want them to grow up coughing and wheezing
as I did
with the toxic dust of war choking the air,
clogging their lungs.
A day comes when you look back,
and the occupation is the only memory you have.
It's your past and future,
your fingerprint.
It is your name.

"I will tell you what is happening here right now.
Just three hours ago,
an Israeli military attack near the border between Gaza and Egypt.
Two Palestinians killed and one Israeli.
And two days ago
when I was walking with a friend

after a wedding celebration,
an air attack targeting a Palestinian car
killed two Palestinians and injured another.

"The children here,
well, it's not really easy to work with them.
Always, always they are thinking about fighting,
about rockets, about tanks, about attacks, about shooting.
They are not thinking about the future.
You know, it's not easy for Palestinian children to think about the
future.
We held a gathering of youth,
fifteen- and sixteen-year olds.
One by one I asked them,
'What are you going to be in the future?'
I was really shocked by their answers,
because most of them said,
'We want to join the resistance.
We want to know how to use weapons and to fight,
to resist the occupation.'
And I was shocked.
'You're not going to think about your future in a positive way?' I asked.
'No,' they said,
'we are just going to join the resistance.'"

Nao Roz, who fought for six months
in the Afghan National Army,
weighs in,
adding his voice to the scales.

"I have little to say,
because it was such a bitter experience,
and now the heaviness of it
is strapped to my back
and never leaves me.
After I left the Army,

it weighed me down,
and, well, there is no other way but to say it:
I tried to kill myself
more than once.

"People think war is a game of numbers—
who is bigger, who is stronger,
who has the most guns.
Easy math,
one side against another.
You think you can play and win.
In Kunar, I fought in a battle.
When it was over,
thirty or forty people were twisted and dead on the ground,
all Afghans.
And I didn't even know why I was there.
Do you hear me?
I didn't know why I was there!
Who decides this Afghan person is with the Taliban
and that Afghan person is a farmer?
And the press couldn't even get the numbers right.
They reported three or four dead
when it was ten times that.
I was there.

"And I was there in Kunar a week later
when a fourteen-year-old bragged
about the fighting he'd done,
the killing he'd seen,
and it was nothing to him,
like pulling weeds
or lighting a cigarette.
He showed me the guns he carried.
And his smile said they were part of his body,
close relations.
When the newspapers measure the war,
will they count him?"

Before we even hear from Cathy Breen in Baghdad
bringing us the voices of Iraqi mothers and teachers—
"Children eight and ten years old think of weapons and killing.
They do not have the thoughts of children.
They all want to be police and carry guns.
I am afraid for my children growing up in this atmosphere"—
the scales tip toward darkness in Afghanistan,
the sun heads south in Palestine,
the day shrinks.

It Must Be Said: A Binding Resolution

Whereas,
it is recognized that objectivity is a hallmark
of professional journalism; and,

Whereas,
it is also understood that objectivity doesn't preclude
personal and editorial decisions about what stories to cover,
their tone and texture, how wide the camera angle,
how close, how detailed the portraits; and,

Whereas,
the media flocked to Newtown, Connecticut
and set up camp there for weeks,
in the wake of the horrific killing
of twenty children at Sandy Hook Elementary school; and,

Whereas,
journalists and bloggers baited us with pictures
of the children and their parents,
hooked us with personal stories,
and drew us in with interviews and intimate accounts
until we felt we were part of the drama; and,

Whereas,
during the first six months of 2012
at least 231 Afghan children were killed in the war,
and 347 were injured; and,

Whereas,
on November 12 in Logar Province, Afghanistan,
a US drone strike killed three children
who were working on the family carrot farm; and,

Whereas,
on October 20, again in Logar Province,
a NATO airstrike killed four boys
who were tending their livestock; and,

Whereas,
on June 6,
yet again in Logar Province,
a US aerial bombardment killed seven women and twelve children,
including a ten-month-old baby and five young girls
all gathered to celebrate a wedding; and,

Whereas,
the week before, in Paktia Province,
a US drone strike killed six children and two women; and,

Whereas,
three weeks earlier in Helmand Province,
a US warplane killed five children and a woman; and,

Whereas,
in November, 2012,
during a hideous eight-day Israeli military assault on Gaza,
33 Palestinian children were killed,
247 were injured, and many more were traumatized; and,

Whereas,
the Afghan and Palestinian children
were ignored on television
and rarely presented in the press; and,

Whereas,
no flock of journalists migrated to Gaza
to document the lives of these children and their families,
no barrage of reports came to us from Paktia or Helmand or Logar,
no pictures of the children

to evoke a sympathetic response,
to help us view them as our own,
no interviews with their parents or their friends or their teachers,
no blogosphere lit up by stories of their interests, their ambition, their
potential
cut short.

Therefore,
it must be said.

Therefore, finally,
be it concluded,
that some children matter
more than others.

GAZA

A Palestinian girl on a Gaza rooftop. November, 2012.

Strength, Suffering, Courage, and Resilience

a comment by David Smith-Ferri

A series of foreign interventions and military occupation—beginning with British rule ninety years ago and continuing through Egyptian and Israeli occupations—have scarred the political, social, and economic history of the Gaza Strip. Most recently, in November 2012, the Israel Defense Forces (IDF) launched an eight-day naval and aerial assault on this 140 square-mile Palestinian territory, where more than 1.7 million people live in conditions of daily humiliation and social injustice sometimes compared to apartheid.

Technically, the Palestinian people in Gaza govern themselves through the Muslim political organization Hamas, but Israel controls their airspace, territorial waters, and border crossings as well as the main supplies of water and electricity. Israeli checkpoints within Gaza and on its international borders severely limit travel and access, separate families, choke economic activity, and demean Palestinians, who cannot legally leave the Gaza Strip without permission.

By its own count, the IDF attacked over fifteen hundred sites during what it called Operation Pillar of Defense (literally translated from the Hebrew as Operation Pillar of Cloud). IDF missiles damaged or destroyed Palestinian homes, businesses, mosques, hospitals, bridges, roads, health clinics, government buildings, schools, and orchards. According to statistics maintained by the Palestinian Center for Human Rights, 156 Palestinians, including 103 civilians, died in these attacks, and 971 civilians were injured.

For their part, Palestinian armed groups carry out incursions against Israel including rocket attacks and assaults on Israeli soldiers. They launched rocket attacks in the weeks leading up to Operation Pillar of Defense. Between November 14 and November 21, 2012, they launched nearly fifteen hundred rockets at Israel. More than eight hundred rockets struck Israeli soil. Many landed in open areas, but some reached suburban or urban neighborhoods, damaging homes, schools, and buildings, killing five Israeli civilians and injuring more than two hundred.

Violence by each side in the conflict reinforces violence by the other and qualifies as a justification for retaliation. When Israel launched its attack on Gaza, three members of Voices for Creative Nonviolence–Josh Brollier, Johnny Barber, and Kathy Kelly–left for the region. They were able to enter Gaza, arriving in the country two days after the November 21 ceasefire. Josh had this to say about his reasons for traveling to Gaza:

I felt disgusted and enraged watching the news as Israel's Pillar of Cloud assault began to unfold. It reminded me too much of 2008-2009, when more than fourteen hundred Palestinians were killed in twenty-two days by Israeli forces in Operation Cast Lead, and world powers did nothing in response. I watched that New Years' massacre on Al-Jazeera and felt sick to my stomach the entire time. I then participated in a sit-in protest at Senator Durbin's office demanding that funding be revoked from the Israeli military for carrying out such atrocities, but Senator Durbin and practically no one in the US Congress, including President-elect Barack Obama, wanted to speak out against what Israel was doing.

This time in 2012, I decided I couldn't watch a similar scenario unfold. I wanted to be with the people of Gaza in their struggle, and tell their stories directly, without the filter of news agencies like the BBC or even Aljazeera. Amidst all the heartbreaking stories and widespread destruction, I immediately fell in love with the people of Gaza and their resilient determination to live with dignity despite the isolation of the siege and such massive, indiscriminate assaults from Israel. "Collective punishment" is a term often thrown around in human rights and international law circles. And in Gaza, it remains to be seen what crime the 1.7 million Palestinians are guilty of committing other than their "collective existence" in the face of blatant apartheid and routine military harassment by the Israeli government. I felt honored in having the opportunity to stand with my sisters and brothers in Palestine against such madness.

Reporting by Kathy, Josh, and Johnny drew us into the lives of Palestinian people at a time when their country was under attack. It educated us about the consequences of Israeli missile attacks, introduced us to Palestinian families trapped beneath a rain of missiles, and reminded us that real people lay behind the media fog of military strategies, prognostications, and statistics. The poems that follow, based on the reports, are another effort to render clearly the consequences of war. With the poems, I want to portray the people who suffer these consequences as more than victims.

Reporting with empathy about Palestinian experiences—whether in the form of an editorial, article, or lecture—draws criticism as "unbalanced." A problem with the critique is that imbalance is at the root of the relationship between Israel and Palestine. There is, to start, the massive difference in Palestinian and Israeli military capabilities and the disproportionate consequences of their military actions. Difference extends to significant disparities in social, economic, and political influence and power. Another gap is clearly evidenced in the vastly greater amount of US aid to Israel compared to US aid to Palestine.

Emerging from encounters with people in Gaza, the poetry focuses on the present-day strength, suffering, courage, and resilience of Palestinian people. If the poems are effective in communicating some of this, I will be as pleased with the poems as I am grateful to my friends at Voices for Creative Nonviolence for their travel to war zones and their efforts to amplify the voices of people that most often remain unheard.

Rubble of the al-Dalu family home where ten people, including four young children, died. Nasser Street, Gaza City, Gaza

—photo by Johnny Barber

At approximately 15:30, Israeli warplanes fired two missiles at two cars that were traveling in the al-Sabra neighborhood, in which five civilians were traveling. As a result of this attack, five civilians were killed: Subhi Nemer Mohammed Dughmosh, twenty-nine; Salah Nember Mohammed Dughmosh, twenty-nine; Ahmed Jameel Hamdan Dughmosh, thirty; Zaki Saeed Mohammed Qadada, forty-two; and Mosab Mahmoud Rushdi Dughmosh, twenty-five.

—Palestinian Human Rights Center website

Everything

During the eight-day siege of Gaza,
no person,
no place
was off limits.
Israel's military tornado touched down
when and wherever it chose.
As Hazem Jamal Nasser,
a young Palestinian
whose brother was killed by a missile,
put it,
"They want to clear everything."
Meaning,
schools, ambulances, mosques, bridges,
mothers, fathers, children, grandparents
past, present, future.
Even people driving home from a funeral,
mourners,
people with one foot in this world
and one temporarily in the next
were sucked into the vortex
and swept away.

"My brother Zaki was targeted
for no reason,"
said Saad Qadada,
"just like the al-Dalu family

and anyone else who is civilian.
My brother had seven children.
I will take care of them,
but it's not the same,
not the same as having your father.
A father is half of everything."

Only Farmers, Only Families

Firhas's parents speak

Firhas was not in the wrong place.
This wasn't random
or unavoidable.
It wasn't bad luck.
Firhas was exactly where an eight-year-old boy should be
at midnight:
asleep in his bed.
The missiles had no right,
no right to be here.
But they came anyway,
cutting off the electricity
so we had to move,
terrified
in darkness,
using a mobile phone light
to find our children.
They screamed for us.
Smoke filled their room,
and blood spattered the walls.
Their blood.
The explosion shattered windows,
and to reach our children,
we choked and stumbled
barefoot
on glass.
Shrapnel had torn through two walls.
It tore through our younger son's leg
and Firhas's neck,
decapitating him,
leaving his headless body
to fall on top of his younger sister.
Firhas, who loved games.
Firhas, who was a little naughty

but kind.
Firhas, who was the generator of our house.
An eight-year-old boy.
They executed him.

We had to carry two of our children
out of their room
and out of the house
because they were in shock.
And our daughter Leila wouldn't speak.

It had been quiet in Beit Hanoun.
There was no one living here
that you could call a terrorist.
Only farmers.
Only families.
But terror came anyway.
It came from outside.
It moved uninvited into our home.
And it lives now
like cancer
in the minds
and bodies
of our children.

After

Unlike their feathered namesake, mechanical falcons—
F-16s favored today for aerial bombardments—
fly at night.
And on the night of November 16,
sometime after midnight—
who can be sure now?—
they fired four missiles
at an olive grove in Beit Hanoun
in the northeast corner
of the Gaza strip.

"The weapons used in this war,"
Dr. Tariz said,
"are bigger than Israel used in 2009.
One missile can completely destroy a building."
Shrapnel from these missiles
traveled at least four hundred yards.
And if it sang or whistled while it flew,
no one heard it.

And when workers came to rescue the injured—
four firemen because there were no ambulances available—
another missile met them.

After,
when there should have been so many words,
Leila stood mute on the side.
After,
there was only silence.

Firhas's Seven-Year-Old Sister, Leila

At first,
coming out of a deep sleep,
I thought the missiles
were a bad dream.
Then I wanted them to be.
And even today,
I think
if I just wish hard enough,
my brother's broken body,
flung over mine,
will come back to life.

Always

A part of us had always understood.
For years,
the letters had lain scrambled
in some neglected side passage, pulsing
and rubbing against each other
in a dark quadrant of our minds.
Over time,
we piled rocks in a passageway
imprisoning them.
But still we felt their heat
as they formed words,
and the words gathered together into phrases.
We kept to the wide main chamber
with its high ceiling,
with the fire in the center of its floor
and the great ring of torches
marking its boundaries.
But we knew the words were there
throbbing in the darkness.
At night,
when the fire burned to embers,
we heard them murmuring
and scratching,
trying to climb out.
And we turned uneasily in our sleep.
But it wasn't until we entered the Basyouni family home
in Gaza
and met Leila face to face
that we knew they had formed a sentence,
scaled the rock wall,
and escaped.
Seven-year-old Leila
who woke in bed
to find her eight-year-old brother's decapitated body

thrown across her by a missile.
Leila, who used to have so much to say,
shocked into silence.

Now there is nowhere to hide
from their message
and the question it implies:
War is a horror. Always.
What am I doing to stop
and prevent it?

More Than a Story

after a report by Kathy Kelly

The killing of at least eight members
of the al-Dalu family—
four women and four young children—
was more than a story
before Josh and Kathy and Johnny
entered Gaza City.

It was more than a story
before they stood in front of the impossible pile
of broken concrete and bent steel
that only days before
had been the multi-level al-Dalu apartment building,
still,
it is feared,
holding one missing family member.

The pile is crowned now with an overturned car
heaved by the missile on top
like an afterthought—
or finishing touch.

It was more than a story
before Johnny stood nearby
and photographed a shiny plastic banner.
Hung beside the wreckage,
the banner portrays seven-year-old Sarah,
six-year-old Jamal, four-year-old Youssef,
and one-year-old Ibrahim,
their enlarged color close-up portraits
floating on a sky-blue background.

The blue banner
stands out against gray cinder block.

It ripples in the breeze.
It wraps their faces in color
as their family had wrapped them in love.
The children look right at us.
Almost close enough to touch,
if only time were more fluid,
if only Mr. al-Dalu,
who survived,
could reach his hands back through it,
as through water,
just a few days' distance.
If only he could coax them
and their mother and grandmother
and great-grandmother
out of their home
for a short walk
before the missile strikes.

It was more than a story
before we met twenty-nine-year-old Mahmoud,
Mr. al-Dalu's nephew.
Before he told us
that he and his family
had moved out of the apartment building
only weeks ago
into a building next door
he'd built himself.
A new home,
where preparations for a birthday party
for their two-year-old daughter were underway
and where one ruined wall now lays
still garlanded by ribbon.

It was more than a story
before Mahmoud wiped his hand across his brow
and looked us in the eyes:

"I don't know why this happened to us.
I am a pharmacist.
In my uncle's house lived a doctor
and a computer engineer.
We were just finishing lunch.
There were no terrorists here.
Only family members.
Now I don't know what to do,
where to go.
We are living in misery."

It was more than a story
before Kathy told it,
entitling it,
"Truth and Trauma in Gaza."
Now we know.

There Was Nothing I Could Do

Haneen's mother speaks

It happened that quickly.
Haneen Khaled,
my first-born,
my only child,
broken.
Why did they do it?
Tell me,
tell me why they did it!
Tell me why I had to pick
my baby's broken body up
from the floor?

Only last week,
our house stood,
and I stood
watching Haneen.
Sunlight filled the room,
and I saw him in front of me.
He had just learned to pull himself up,
to stand.
Every day he dreamed of walking.
It was his idea.
An explorer
preparing for a journey,
he was a great thinker
puzzling out the steps.
Who knew how far he could go?

Sunday, November 17, 2012, Central Gaza: At approximately 20:30, Israeli warplanes attacked a number of civilians who gathered at a plot belonging to Ahmed Salem Bin Saeed, fifty-two, when they heard that one of his relatives was killed. As a result of the attack, Bin Saeed and Hani Abdul Majid Buraiem, thirty-one, were killed, and six others were wounded.

—Palestinian Center for Human Rights website

Backroom Military Strategy

One grief is never enough.
One grief could unify people.
One grief,
like a patch on torn clothes,
could cover fear,
strengthen resistance.
One grief could remind people
who they are,
what they have.
But lay one grief on top of another,
and they multiply each other.
Build the pile high enough,
and the whole community,
the whole Gaza strip
will fray,
unravel,
tear at its seams.

Time

following reports by the Palestinian Center for Human Rights

In Gaza,
time has stopped.
Hearts still beat,
trees flower, and hands harvest their fruit.
Eyes open, shut, and open again.
The sun still travels overhead
and melts into the Mediterranean Sea.
But time has stopped.

On one street in the al-Sabra neighborhood of Gaza City,
it stopped on Tuesday, November 20
when lightning from a blue sky incinerated two cars.
The time was 3:30 pm,
and their five passengers
were traveling home from a funeral.
One cause for grief wasn't enough.
They never heard the twin blasts of thunder
that rocked the neighborhood,
that still ring in the ears of its residents.

Around midnight on November 16,
four missiles rained down,
causing a massive landslide
that dammed the free-flowing river of time
and flooded a neighborhood east of Beit Hanoun,
killing two Palestinian children
and destroying five homes and a mosque.
Twenty-two civilians,
including fourteen women and three children,
were injured in the flood.

In a Beit Lahia housing project,
time stopped on November 18

at 1:50 in the morning
when an Israeli warplane
bombed a four-story house,
destroying it
along with five neighboring houses,
five shops,
five cars,
two trucks,
and a bus.

Ten minutes later,
time stopped in Jabalya
east of Tal al-Zatar
when a missile destroyed a house
belonging to the Eseifan family,
killing two children—
Tamer, age four
and Jumana, age two.

The next day
nearby
in the Ebad al-Rahman neighborhood,
time stopped at 2:10 pm,
when an Israeli drone
fired a missile
into the garden of a house,
killing twenty-nine-year old Ayman,
twelve-year-old Abeer,
and their father.

In al-Mansoura Street
at dawn,
in the al-Shujaiya neighborhood,

Sadiya al-Dib's wife
was feeding chickens in the garden
when a missile stopped time.

East of Khan Yunis
in the Abu Nasser area in Abassan village,
farmers were harvesting olives
on November 19.
Time stopped with the sun straight overhead,
when a missile killed Ibrahim Abu Nasser
and his fourteen-year-old granddaughter, Ameera.

The day before
in al-Qarara village,
it stopped in mid-morning
when a missile struck an olive grove,
killing two-year-old Waleed al-Abadla.

North of Rafah
in the al-Shaboura refugee camp,
time stopped on November 18
in the cold hours before dawn
when Ahmed Abu Nuqaira and his family
were frantically evacuating their home
after the Israeli military fired warning missiles
at a nearby house belonging to a member of an armed group.
Before the terrified family could flee,
a missile struck,
killing Ahmed.

In every neighborhood in Gaza,
time has stopped.
In every neighborhood,

it is a different day or hour.
But the rest of the world
continues to roll forward,
getting farther and farther
away,
and Gaza—
a small strip of land in the first place—
recedes
until once again we can barely see it.

We Asked the Media For People

We asked for vigorous reporting,
and they gave us tired words,
an endless desert of bloodless words,
words like sand,
sand in our ears and eyes.

We asked for stories,
and they gave us statistics—
the percentage of missiles
stopped by Israel's Iron Dome,
the distance the farthest-reaching Hamas rockets can travel.

We asked for people,
and they gave us numbers—
the increase or decrease
in the quantity of rockets
fired by Hamas
compared to the previous two- or three-day period,
the number of Israeli ground troops
massing on the border of Gaza.

We asked for mouths and eyes,
for hands—
and they stared at us.

We asked for faces,
and they turned their backs
and walked away.

Palestinian Center for Human Rights'
Weekly Report on Israeli Human Rights Violations
in the Occupied Territories

A long list.
Line after line
of black words
on white pages.
Between the lines,
blood red,
gray despair,
blue hope,
aquamarine compassion,
flaming defiance.
Every color
on the planet.

Mohammad Bakr

after a story related by Josh Brollier

the Israel Defense Force speaks

What are we going to do
with these Palestinian fishermen?
We force them
at gunpoint
to strip
and jump into icy water
miles from shore,
but they surface,
bobbing like corks,
unsinkable.

From helicopter gunships and naval vessels,
we fire into the engines
of their boats,
but they haul them away
and repair them.
The same boats,
back from the dead,
hum again
and churn these waters.

And today,
with fishermen
on a half dozen other boats as his witness,
Mohammad Bakr
looked straight into our gun barrels
and refused to blink,
refused to strip.
"You can put a bullet in my head
before I will jump into the water."
He draped his body
like a shield

over the engine.
Our guns lay limp in our hands.
We stood naked in sunshine,
and the eyes of the other fishermen,
sparkling like the sea at noon,
watched
as his boat steered around us.

The name of the Israeli military operation in Gaza is based on the pillar of cloud that accompanied the nation of Israel during the Exodus as they left Egypt and were traveling toward Israel. They wanted protection from the troubles of the desert, from robbers and people that would attack them, and from snakes and scorpions. The name is meant to send the message that it is a defensive maneuver.

—Eytan Buchman, head of the North American media desk for
the Israel Defense Forces

Six days into the aerial attack on Gaza, eighty-four percent of the Israeli public supports Operation Pillar of Defense (Operation Pillar of Cloud), with twelve percent opposing it, according to a Haaretz-Dialog poll taken Sunday. The poll surveyed proportional samples of Jews and Arabs, indicating that Jewish support for the war stands at upwards of ninety percent.

—*Haaretz*, November 19, 2012

Operation Pillar of Cloud

The Israeli military's eight-day assault
on the people of Gaza
was no downy pillar of cloud,
no feathered wing
moving lightly across the landscape
defending its chicks,
leading the way
to life.

It was iron talon and hooked beak.
It was switchblade and brass knuckles,
a heavy metal club in the dark
from behind.
It was panes of glass
falling from the sky
to open arteries
and sever limbs.

It was piano wire and guillotine,
a child's blood on the walls.

Which is to say,
it was the same as the 2009 assault,
and the one before that,
and so on.

For something else,
listen to Palestinian ambulance drivers
who arrive at the scenes of missile attacks
and offer a lifeline,
who themselves are targeted by "double taps,"
secondary missile attacks at bomb sites
after rescue workers have arrived.

"I do it," Shadi says,
"for the sake of my country."
And Aadl, who graduated in journalism,
who suffers "until this moment" from PTSD:
"I want to give more and more to my people."

For something different,
listen to Palestinian doctors.
"Part of the problem is psychological . . .
I hate hatred.
We should talk with Israeli people
and learn what they actually want.
Start with the ten percent of Israeli society that is sane
and work from there."

For words that will stop you
in your tracks
and then point the way to life,
listen to the al-Nasser family
whose fifteen-year-old son Odai was killed

in his bed
in the middle of the night
when shrapnel
like a chainsaw
cut him.

Listen to Odai's aunt.
"Over the years,
our neighborhood has been attacked five times.
During their operations,
Israeli soldiers take over my home
and fire on Palestinians from it.
They also urinate in my pots and pans
and defecate nearby in the yard.
I clean up after them
because they won't do it.
When they first arrive,
they use me
as a shield
while they search my house,
even though no one else is in it.
During this most recent attack,
I was locked in my kitchen
for most of the time,
and I had to ask a soldier for permission
before I could use the outdoor restroom.

"There is so much to be sad about.
In Palestine
and in Israel.
We are sad about rockets killing Israelis, too.
We care about their children, too.
Their suffering
and our suffering
are the same."

Acknowledgments

This is the third book collaboration with Marcia Gagliardi. We've become friends in the process. With each project, my respect for her talents and diligence and my gratitude for her guidance have grown

Mary-Ann Palmieri, copy-editor suprema

Theresa Whitehill and Adrienne Simpson of Colored Horse Studios for the beautiful book cover

Kathy Kelly for her friendship, for inviting me to join her on visits to Afghanistan, and for her belief in the poems and their role in educating readers and in the global peace movement we must forge

My friends at Voices for Creative Nonviolence — Buddy Bell, Josh Brollier, and Cathy Breen — for their activism, commitment, and their service

Abdulai Safaari, Johnny Barber, Josh Brollier, and Teck Wee Young for use of their photographs

Ann Wright for her generosity in writing a Foreword

Rangina Hamidi, Mairead MaGuire, and Intimaa Al-Sududi for reading the manuscript and commenting on it

My partner, Sherrie, and our daughter, Rachael, for supporting my writing, and for sharing in the vision of friendship with Afghan people as well as the perils of travel

The members of our local poetry group — Susan, Benj, David, Sue, Lisa, Pam, David, Mary, Theresa, Armand, Jonathan, Darca — for their support and encouragement

The Afghan Peace Volunteers for welcoming me into their home, sharing their lives, offering their friendship

*Poet David Smith-Ferri with Abdulai, a member of the
Afghan Peace Volunteers
—photo by Jerica Arents*

About the Author

David Smith-Ferri grew up in an Italian-Irish family in a suburb of
New York City. His mother's love for the literary and other arts and
her keen sense of justice shaped his sensibilities. As an undergraduate
at Boston College participating in its service-learning program, he
worked in inner-city social service programs. He went on to get an
MSW from the University of Washington and to work as a social
worker in Seattle and New York. It wasn't until he and his then-five-
year-old daughter Rachael began visiting the Plowshares activist Susan
Crane in prison that he began to make connections between poverty
and social injustice in the US and American foreign policy. He has
been active with Voices for Creative Nonviolence (formerly Voices
in the Wilderness) since he first traveled to Iraq in 1999. Poetry has
played an increasingly important part of his activism as he has sought
effective ways to communicate the urgency of the problems he has
witnessed and to represent the voices of those who bear the brunt
of the US-led wars on Iraq and Afghanistan. He has two other books
of poetry published by Haley's, *Battlefield without Borders* and *With
Children Like Your Own*. He lives in northern California with his wife
and daughter. He can be reached at dsmithferri@gmail.com.

Colophon

Text, titles, captions, and other type for *When Dayts Are Stone* are set in Gill Sans, a sans-serif typeface designed by Eric Gill.

The original design appeared in 1926 when Douglas Cleverdon opened a bookshop in his home town of Bristol, England, where Gill painted the fascia over the window in sans-serif capitals that would later be known as Gill Sans.

Gill further developed the font into a complete family after Stanley Morison commissioned the development of Gill Sans to combat the families of Erbar, Futura, and Kabel, launched in Germany during the late 1920s. Gill Sans was later released in 1928 by Monotype Corporation.

Gill was a well established sculptor, graphic artist, and type designer, and the Gill Sans typeface takes inspiration from Edward Johnston's Johnston typeface for London Underground, which Gill had worked on while apprenticed to Johnston. Gill attempted to make the ultimate legible sans-serif text face.

The letter *a* was originally developed with a straight tail, followed by a diagonal tail (which can be seen on early specimen sheets), then the hooked tail.

The original Gill Sans lacked distinctions between numeral *1*, uppercase *i*, and lowercase *L*, so an alternate version of Gill Sans was made that included an alternate *1* that could be used for numerical settings.

Gill removed terminus endings of the vertical stroke in *b, d, p,* and *q,* but the Monotype drawing office revised the forms so that they were preserved in the medium weight.

CPSIA information can be obtained at www.ICGtesting.com
Printed in the USA
BVOW05s1529230814

363949BV00003B/8/P